Presented to:

_____

FROM

_____

DATE

the Art of Abundance

A SIMPLE GUIDE TO
DISCOVERING LIFE'S TREASURES

Candy Paull

Stewart, Tabori & Chang
New York

Editor: Marisa Bulzone
Designer: LeAnna Weller Smith
Production Manager: Kim Tyner

Library of Congress Cataloging-in-Publication
Data:

Paull, Candy.
The art of abundance : a simple guide to
discovering life's treasures / by Candy Paull.
      p. cm.
   ISBN 1-58479-445-3
   1. Spiritual life. 2. Wealth. I. Title.

BL624.P38 2006
178--dc22

2005029806

Scripture quotations marked RSV are taken from
The Revised Standard Version of the Bible, copyright
© 1946, Old Testament section copyright © 1952
by the Division of Christian Education of the
Churches of Christ in the United States of
America. Used by permission.

Scripture quotations marked NIV are taken from
the Holy Bible New International Version® NIV®
copyright © 1973, 1978, 1984 by the International
Bible Society. Used by permission of Zondervan
Publishing House. All rights reserved.

Scripture quotations marked KJV are taken from
the King James Version of the Bible.
Originally published in 1998 by Honor Books,
Tulsa, Oklahoma.

Published in 2006 by
Stewart, Tabori & Chang
An imprint of
Harry N. Abrams, Inc.

The text of this book was composed in Corporate S,
Filosofia and Type Embellishments.

Printed and bound in China by
Midas Printing Ltd.
10 9 8 7 6 5 4 3 2 1

HNA ▮▮▮▮ ▮
harry n. abrams, inc.
a subsidiary of La Martinière Groupe

Harry N. Abrams, Inc.
115 West 18th Street
New York, NY 10011
www.hnabooks.com

To my parents
Robert and Ruth Paull
who taught me my first lessons
in the art of abundance

contents

INTRODUCTION

The art of abundance is the art of awareness. It is a way to count our blessings and practice mindfulness in our daily living. Becoming aware of the small, the little, and the least offers us an opportunity to open our hearts to a larger perspective. We learn to value the tastes, textures, scents, sounds, and sights of our lives as they present themselves to us moment by moment.

Children practice the art of abundance naturally, but often as adults we love the ability to explore and experience wonder. By choosing to be aware of the gifts life brings, we become lovers instead of critics, believers instead of doubters, and childlike mystics instead of world-weary cynics.

Practicing the art of abundance has been a transforming process in my life. My spirit has been renewed and my heart refreshed whenever I have chosen to thank the great Creator for the blessings that come my way. It is my prayer that this little book will enable you to affirm the goodness of creation and discover how rich you are in the things that count.

Candy Paull

The Appreciation
of Abundance

I feel an earnest and humble desire, and shall do till I die,

to increase the stock of harmless cheerfulness.

—CHARLES DICKENS

Abundance is . . . not how much I own but
how much I appreciate.

I am come that they might have life,
and that they might have it more abundantly.
—JOHN 10:10 (KJV)

Abundance is . . . a pink and lavender sunset sky.

Abundance is . . . the smell of fresh-baked
chocolate chip cookies.

Abundance is . . . an unexpected phone call from a friend.

The Appreciation of Abundance

Earth's crammed with heaven,
And every common bush afire with God.
—ELIZABETH BARRETT BROWNING

Abundance is . . . a flowerpot full of Red Rubin basil
bursting with exuberant flavor and scent.

Abundance is . . . ruby taillights and diamond headlights
creating a freeway necklace in the dark.

The art of abundance is not about greed or selfishness. The art of abundance is about celebrating life right now, this minute. It is a way of looking at the potential your life holds—the little blessings to be thankful for now and the gifts that God wants to give you, if you'll open your heart to receive them. It's about being enthusiastic about life every day, not just on the rare occasions when everything seems to be going your way.

Write in your heart that every day is the best day of the year.

—RALPH WALDO EMERSON

The art of abundance is finding the provision in what is right in front of you, seeing the hand of God already giving you what you need, moment by moment, sharing the abundant blessings God has given with others, and completing the circle of giving by praising the One who gave the gifts for us to enjoy.

Choice of attention—to pay attention to this and
ignore that—is to the inner life what choice of action
is to the outer. In both cases, a man is responsible for
his choice and must accept the consequences.

—W. H. AUDEN

Abundance is . . . wildflowers in a mason jar.

Abundance is . . . the stars on a clear night.

Be thine own palace, or the world's thy jail.
—JOHN DONNE

Abundance is . . . creating something special
out of the ordinary.

Abundance is . . . the look of wonder in a
two-year-old child's eyes.

Abundance is . . . the first lick of an ice cream cone.

Abundance is . . . cows in clover.

For I know the plans I have for you.
They are plans for your good, not to destroy you or bring evil to you.
These plans are for a future full of hope and promise.
—JEREMIAH 29:11 (AUTHOR'S PARAPHRASE)

17

OVERCOMING FEARS

I first started consciously practicing the art of abundance a few years ago. My parents had always shared their delight in small things—the view from the front window, the comings and goings of birds and wildlife, the pleasure of flowers on the table and well-cooked food, the joy of reading— but it wasn't until I became an adult that I realized how rich their lives have always been in celebrating the small abundances of life.

Abundance is . . . a rich red oriental rug.

Abundance is . . . a vase full of roses from the garden.

Abundance is . . . watching the seasons change outside your window.

As a freelance writer, I've had times of plenty—but I've had a lot more times of doing without, making do, or just plain being frustrated by a short financial leash. And many times of being scared, because I didn't know how my bills were going to get paid. It seemed I could barely manage the basics, let alone the extras.

But when I learned to live the abundant life, I began to feel rich in spite of fluctuating finances. And I firmly believe that most of the improvements in my financial situation have come about because I learned to stop being fearful and start being creatively thankful. By being receptive to the gifts I had already received, greater gifts came more freely. God was at last able to give the gifts He'd been wanting to give me all along.

I also learned how to react to life differently. It didn't come all at once. I didn't suddenly wake up one day and say, "Gee, if I'd just see the glass as half full instead of half empty, I'd enjoy life more." I learned incrementally, one small lesson on top of another small lesson, with the big picture coming slowly into focus.

Once I began to look at life through a more positive lens, I found I had more energy and was able to enjoy the opportunities that came my way because I was no longer blinded by my fear. I could say "yes" to life. I learned that creativity grows in feelings of abundance. And I discovered that my thankfulness for current blessings made me aware of other abundances that I might otherwise have blindly overlooked.

Abundance is . . . having enough for today.

Abundance is . . . a warm bed to fall into when you are tired.

Abundance is . . . pink lemonade.

Abundance is . . . freshly picked red strawberries and
rich white cream in a cobalt blue bowl.

Light tomorrow with today.
—ELIZABETH BARRETT BROWNING

Some wandered in desert wastes, finding no way to a city to dwell in;
hungry and thirsty, their soul fainted within them.
Then they cried to the Lord in their trouble,
and he delivered them from their distress;
he led them by a straight way, till they reached a city to dwell in.
Let them thank the Lord for his steadfast love
for his wonderful works to the sons of men!
For he satisfies him who is thirsty,
and the hungry he fills with good things.

—PSALM 107:4-9 (RSV)

Abundance is . . . ivy and morning glories in a vacant lot.

Abundance is . . . being able to say "yes."

Abundance is . . . being able to say "no."

The happiness of life is made up of minute fractions—
the little soon forgotten charities of a kiss or smile, a kind look,
a heartfelt compliment, and the countless infinitesimals
of pleasurable and genial feeling.

—SAMUEL TAYLOR COLERIDGE

Abundance is . . . a sunny day when you
expected stormy weather.

Abundance is . . . the first page of a new novel
from a favorite author.

Abundance is . . . a full moon playing
hide-and-seek with the clouds.

Always leave enough time in your life to do something
that makes you happy, satisfied, even joyous. That has more of an
effect on economic well-being than any other single factor.
—PAUL HAWKEN

Abundance is . . . nurturing a tiny seedling.

Abundance is . . . bath time for little ones.

Abundance is . . . a child learning her ABCs.

Abundance is . . . being able to read this page.

Only the individual with a healthy, wholesome self-view will feel inwardly rich when he or she is outwardly broke.

—MARSHA SINETAR

The Appreciation of Abundance

Truth exists for the wise, beauty for the feeling heart.

—JOHANN VON SCHILLER

Abundance is . . . the ability to look at life with the eyes
of an appreciative lover.

*In every man's heart there is a secret nerve that answers
to the vibrations of beauty.*

—CHRISTOPHER MORLEY

Abundance is . . . taking the long scenic route home.

The strength and happiness of a man consists in finding out the
way in which God is going, and going in that way too.
—HENRY WARD BEECHER

Abundance is . . . pigeons flying into a church bell tower.

Abundance is . . . a cat purring on your lap.

Abundance is . . . freshly popped popcorn.

Blessed is everyone that feareth the LORD; that walketh
in his ways. For thou shalt eat the labour of thine hands;
happy shalt thou be, and it shall be well with thee.
—PSALM 128:1-2 (KJV)

Abundance is . . . the face of someone who has survived
the storms of life with faith and gratitude.

Abundance is . . . a dance studio full of eager little ballerinas.

Happiness lies in the absorption in some vocation which satisfies the soul.
—HENRY WARD BEECHER

Abundance is . . . a box of crayons and a clean sheet of paper.

Abundance is . . . a bouquet of fresh flowers and
a vase to arrange them in.

Whatever your task, work heartily, as serving the Lord and not men.
—COLOSSIANS 3:23 (RSV)

Abundance is . . . a piano recital where
parents are as nervous watching as
the children are performing.

A NEW WAY OF LOOKING AT LIFE

In some ways I consider practicing the art of abundance as a way of practicing the art of seeing. Artists train themselves to really look at the world around them. And they don't see through everybody else's frame of reference. They discover their own unique vantage point and then express what they've seen in creative ways.

That's what this little book is all about. It's a visual aid, a spiritual tool for learning to look at your own life in healing, creative ways. It is a way to cultivate opportunity for observation and practice the discipline of simple thankfulness to the Creator. When I practice seeing and experiencing my life through the lens of hope and gratitude, I find that life expands in new and unexpected ways.

P racticing the art of abundance means looking at the world as it is, right in front of you, not as you think it should be. It is a way of letting go of expectations and letting what is, what already exists, speak to you in a new way.

Abundance is . . . an old hound dog dozing on the porch.

Abundance is . . . a pair of warm hazel eyes.

The world is God's language to us.

—SIMONE WEIL

Abundance is . . . the velvet petals of a newly opened flower.

Abundance is . . . chicks in an incubator.

Abundance is . . . a maternity ward.

Look at the lilies and the way they grow. They do not toil.
They do not spin. Yet I tell you, even King Solomon in all his
glory was never dressed as wonderfully as these.
—LUKE 12:27 (AUTHOR'S PARAPHRASE)

Abundance is . . . tall, tall redwoods creating
a hushed mountain cathedral.

Abundance is . . . a pink rose surrounded
by a constellation of baby's breath.

Abundance is . . . an art gallery full of paintings.

Art is the demonstration that the ordinary is extraordinary.
—AMEDEE OZENFANT

Abundance is . . . an afternoon in a meadow with
canvas, easel, paintbrush—and butterflies!

Abundance is . . . the first daffodils of spring.

Abundance is . . . white clouds dancing across the sky.

Abundance is . . . paying attention to
the moment here and now.

Abundance is . . . the swish of clear,
clean water from a faucet.

One of the most important—and most neglected—
elements in the beginnings of the interior life is the ability
to respond to reality, to see the value and the beauty in
ordinary things, to come alive to the splendor
that is all around us in the creatures of God.

—THOMAS MERTON

The Appreciation of Abundance

Abundance is . . . a windowbox of purple and gold pansies.

Abundance is . . . a slice of moon in a cold winter sky.

Abundance is . . . crisp, shiny apples on a fall afternoon.

Abundance is . . . an exercise class to stretch and tone your body.

Abundance is . . . a white wicker chair on a shady porch.

Every believer must be a kind of psalmist,
either literally or privately. That living itself has been given,
at least in part, as a way of knowing God intimately.
Every event takes on a significance in that context,
for there is no waste in experience.
—PHYLLIS A. TICKLE, *WHAT THE HEART ALREADY KNOWS*

Abundance is . . . a pure white mountain peak
rising above wildflower meadows.

The Appreciation of Abundance

Abundance is . . . fireflies twinkling like stars on the lawn.

Abundance is . . . the salt-smell of an ocean breeze.

Abundance is . . . a hawk making lazy circles in the sky.

EXPECTATIONS, SURPRISES, AND TRUE ABUNDANCE

L etting go of expectations is a big part of the art of abundance. Expectations dictate the way we think abundance should come to us—what kind of box life is supposed to come in. But that limits what God can do in our lives, because He is a God of surprise and diversity and wonder. The only boxes God likes are surprise packages! Our box of expectations labeled "what should be" can often become a trap. True abundance welcomes the surprises of life.

> *If you want total security, go to prison. There you're fed, clothed,*
> *given medical care and so on. The only thing lacking . . . is freedom.*
> —DWIGHT D. EISENHOWER

Without risk, faith is impossible.

—SOREN KIERKEGAARD

Anyone who has taken a look at the zillions of different kinds of bugs or fish or birds or trees or landscapes or noses or animals is reminded of a world so filled with diversity and glorious variety that it becomes obvious our minds cannot contain all that God has created.

The art of abundance is opening my eyes to see what God has lavished on me every single day that I am still breathing. Seeing His abundant surprises at every turn, I am able to open the door to hope and be released from fear, limitation, poverty, and diminished expectation—because God is bigger than my little boxes.

Abundance is . . . a butterfly landing in an outstretched hand.

Abundance more than a mental game of, "If I think hard enough and positively enough I can make what I desire happen." No, it is about seeing that God is good, life is rich, and there are more mysteries of hope and possibility than you could ever dream up yourself.

Abundance is opening to the possibility that what we desire can happen, but also being open to our desires changing and our horizons widening. Instead of trying to dictate how things should come to us, we open our hands and allow life to bring its gifts when and where it will.

Abundance is . . . rich brown soil turned and
waiting for seeds to be planted.

Abundance is . . . changing cloud patterns
in a bright blue sky.

Abundance is . . . a card in the mail from a friend.

God always gives us strength enough, and sense enough,
for everything He wants us to do.
—JOHN RUSKIN

Abundance is . . . renting a three-hanky
romance video and having a good cry.

Go on working, freely and furiously, and you will make progress.
—PAUL GAUGUIN

Abundance is . . . making plans for a summer vacation.

Abundance is . . . a hooked rug your mother
made especially for you.

Abundance is . . . a squirrel skittering down the
side of a tree with a nut in its mouth.

Fear not, little flock; for it is your Father's good pleasure
to give you the kingdom.
—LUKE 12:32 (KJV)

Abundance is . . . licking the beaters.

Abundance is . . . a lazy summer afternoon.

One key to abundant living is to decide to stake my life on the belief that God is good and wants good for me, that He wants to release me from my prison of unfulfilled desire, and make me a person more whole and wonderful than I can even imagine. That's the starting point. To choose to believe that God is good and wants my good. Then to stake my life on it by acting that way.

A small way to do this is to start counting my blessings and begin to see what I've passed over in my rush to solve my problems and find some "perfect" solution to meet my needs. God has a better (and often unexpected) solution, if I will open my hands and my heart to welcome what He wants to bring to me.

Abundance is . . . crayon yellow and orange day lilies.

Abundance is . . . a fresh spring breeze coming
through the bedroom window.

Abundance is . . . bare feet on a summer day.

Happiness is neither within us only, or without us;
it is the union of ourselves with God.

—BLAISE PASCAL

Abundance is . . . honey on whole wheat toast.

Abundance is . . . a long, sensuous kiss.

Abundance is . . . red Jell-O wiggling in a yellow bowl.

Abundance is . . . a vegetable stand at harvest time.

Abundance is . . . the sun breaking through the
clouds on a gloomy day.

Abundance is . . . being early for an appointment.

Abundance is . . . church bells ringing on a Sunday morning.

One of the hardest lessons we have to learn in this life,
and one that many persons never learn, is to see the divine,
the celestial, the pure, in the common, the near at hand—
to see that heaven lies about us here in this world.
—JOHN BURROUGHS

Abundance is . . . cherry and apple blossoms in the spring.

The Appreciation of Abundance

How precious is your unfailing love!
The children and the adults,
all take refuge in the shadow of your wings.
They feast on the abundance of your house;
you give them drink from your river of delights.
For with you is the fountain of life;
in your light do we see light.

—PSALM 36:7-9 (AUTHOR'S PARAPHRASE)

If we did but know how little some enjoy of the great things that
they possess, there would not be much envy in the world.

—EDWARD YOUNG

Abundance is . . . friends knocking at the door.

Abundance is . . . a dog lying on the grass,
waiting for you to scratch his stomach.

The Appreciation of Abundance

Abundance is . . . Japanese lanterns around a patio.

Abundance is . . . a fluffy bath towel.

Abundance is . . . a cup of tea and a moment of quiet.

Abundance is . . . a favorite teddy bear who survived childhood
and now has an honored place in the home.

Abundance is . . . a tender touch where it hurts.

You need not cry very loud; he is nearer to us than we think.
—BROTHER LAWRENCE

Abundance is . . . sunset behind a mountain peak.

Abundance is . . . the laughter of good friends.

Abundance is . . . starlight after a storm.

Let us be of good cheer, remembering that the misfortunes
hardest to bear are those which never happen.

—JAMES RUSSELL LOWELL

A cheerful heart is good medicine, but a broken spirit
makes you feel dry down to your very bones.
—PROVERBS 17:22 (AUTHOR'S PARAPHRASE)

I will bless her with abundant provisions;
her poor will I satisfy with food.
—PSALM 132:15 (NIV)

Abundance is . . . a bag of groceries.

Abundance is . . . electricity being restored after a storm.

SAY NO TO FEAR, SAY YES TO LIFE

I speak from experience. I spent most of my twenties either under-employed or unemployed. It's amazing how stupid a smart woman can be. All my good grades in school never prepared me for the fact that most of life must be taken on faith.

I have learned that it's your view of yourself, your ability to take risks on your own behalf, and your openness to positive change that make the good things happen. I was so busy being fearful, worrying about how bad things were or could be, that I missed out on the good things.

When I began to act on the premise that God wanted good for me, I found that letting go and leaping into that belief began to free me from the box of poverty and fear that I had placed myself in.

The Art of Abundance

O ver the years, I have found that when I practice the art of abundance, I say "no" to my fears and live in today's provision. In the process, I am able to believe in tomorrow's unseen provision, and I am receptive to new and beneficent influences in my life. I know this works. In the long run, I don't really know exactly how it works. But I don't need to know how any more. I don't need to have all the answers. I just need to receive the help that God wants to offer me today.

The art of abundance provides a way for me to open my heart to receive whatever gifts the day itself wants to bring. When I am faithful to doing that, life showers me today with so much more than I could have believed possible in my doubting yesterdays.

Abundance is . . . the sound of rain on a roof that doesn't leak.

Abundance is . . . a book of love poems.

Abundance is . . . a colorful fruit plate.

Everything we are given and everything we are deprived
of is nothing but a finger pointing out the direction of God's
hidden promise which we shall taste in full.

—HENRI NOUWEN

Abundance is . . . earthworms tunneling in the dirt.

Abundance is . . . the first warm day of spring.

God has given some gifts to the whole human race,
from which no one is excluded.

—SENECA

Abundance is . . . freshly laundered clothing.

Abundance is . . . weeds and wild things growing in a field.

Abundance is . . . lying on your back on
the grass and counting stars.

Abundance is . . . little yappy dogs barking with
crazed frenzy as they protect their territory.

Abundance is . . . the aroma of his aftershave
and the scent of her perfume.

Abundance is . . . new shoes.

You hear, O Lord, the desire of the afflicted;
you encourage them, and you listen to their cry.
—PSALM 10:17 (NIV)

Abundance is . . . families picnicking in
the park on a sunny Saturday.

Abundance is . . . a colorful kite flying
high in a windy March sky.

The Appreciation of Abundance

Abundance is . . . someone to kiss goodnight.

And God is able to provide you with every blessing
in abundance, so that you may always have enough of everything
and may provide in abundance for every good work.
—II CORINTHIANS 9:8 (RSV)

Life was meant to be lived, and curiosity must be kept alive.
One must never, for any reason, turn one's back on life.
—ELEANOR ROOSEVELT

The Celebration of Abundance

Each one sees what he carries in his heart.

—GOETHE

CELEBRATE THE ABUNDANT LIFE

As you master simple, practical things to nurture abundance, you will discover new avenues through which you can receive and enjoy and be thankful for the gift of life.

Venture forth and develop your own creative response by seeing the small gifts life gives. I can almost guarantee that if you take even one baby step, you will find a response in the universe, an embracing and a joyous welcome from the Father to a prodigal child who has wasted so many precious hours of life worrying about what was lacking and being blind to the loving abundance all around her.

God bless you as you begin your personal pilgrimage into the kingdom of abundance. Come celebrate the abundant life!

Abundance is . . . children and puppies rolling in the grass.

May your laughter be from God.
—IRISH PROVERB

Abundance is . . . citronella keeping bugs
away on a summer night.

Abundance is . . . a door that opens to let you in.

Abundance is . . . macaroni and cheese
when you want comfort food.

Reflect upon your present blessings, of which every man has many; not on your past misfortunes, of which all men have some.
—CHARLES DICKENS

Abundance is . . . a rest stop on a long hike.

Abundance is . . . a Little League baseball game
on a soft spring afternoon.

Gratitude is born in hearts that take time to count up past mercies.
—CHARLES E. JEFFERSON

Happiness is itself a kind of gratitude.

—JOSEPH WOOD KRUTCH

Abundance is . . . a fresh coat of paint.

Abundance is . . . bare branches against the winter sunset.

He who supplies seed to the sower and bread for food will supply and multiply your resources and increase the harvest of your righteousness.

—II CORINTHIANS 9:10 (RSV)

Abundance is . . . an hour before it's time for bed.

ABUNDANCE IS . . .

C elebrating abundance is the best antidote I know of for fear: fear that whispers there won't be enough for tomorrow, fear that hisses "things will never improve," fear that dominates and tortures, telling you that you're helpless and God has forgotten you. Don't believe it.

Start looking at what you already have. Start with basics like, "I'm still breathing." Make a game seeing how many positives there are in your life. Then start counting the little things, the tiny joys a moment can bring. Open your eyes to see the wonder of the world you live in. I call this the "Abundance is . . ." game. Here is a sampling:

The Celebration of Abundance

Abundance is . . . a cool breeze on a summer evening.

Abundance is . . . a song to sustain you through a dark night.

Abundance is . . . blue jays fighting over the birdseed
in a bird feeder.

Abundance is . . . ginger cookies that snap.

Abundance is . . . the opening chords of the Hallelujah Chorus.

Abundance is . . . warm hands on a cold winter day.

Abundance is . . . someone who asks how you're doing
(and really wants to know!).

Abundance is . . . the smell of a steak sizzling on a
neighbor's barbecue.

Abundance is . . . a cat basking in the sun.

Abundance is . . . a can opener that really works.

Abundance is . . . a white church steeple against a bright blue sky.

Abundance is . . . a flock of geese winging their
way south on a sunny fall day.

Abundance is . . . the first day of a long vacation.

Abundance is . . . the feel of a fine tool in your hand.

Abundance is . . . the sharp smell of fallen pine needles.

Abundance is . . . the opening scene of a favorite movie.

Abundance is . . . all the different noses on all the different faces in the world.

Abundance is . . . walking into a public library.

Abundance is . . . a busy airport.

Abundance is . . . browsing in a fabric store.

Abundance is . . . when you get more than you anticipated.

Abundance is . . . sunlight creating rainbows as it shines through a crystal prism.

Abundance is . . . an understanding friend.

Abundance is . . . dandelion seeds blowing in the wind.

Abundance is . . . a thankful heart.

Abundance is . . . _____(make up your own!)

S tart playing this celebratory game by looking at your life. It's not only the little things to be thankful for. It's the things that illustrate potential.

Abundance . . . is a full tank of gas.

Abundance is . . . a tree loaded with apple blossoms.

Abundance is . . . a telephone line that's connected.

Abundance is . . . flour, sugar, butter, salt, eggs, a recipe, and a kitchen to bake a cake in.

Abundance is . . . a smiling four-year-old.

Abundance is . . . a box full of kittens.

Abundance is . . . an hour to play in the park on a sunny day.

Abundance is . . . the first day you feel better after having the flu.

Abundance is . . . a crocus peeking its head out of the snow.

Abundance is . . . the little, tight, green buds of spring.

CREATING AND CELEBRATING AN ABUNDANT LIFE

Never underestimate the power of celebrating little things. Greet each moment and become aware of what is happening around you. A soft breeze caressing your skin and ruffling the pages of your book. A blue sky outside the window. Or the sound of rain making a murmuring background to your thoughts. The fact that you're enjoying a pleasure, however great or small.

Clean clothes. A hot bath. A smile from a stranger. Lunch hour browsing in the shops. A quick sandwich on the run. Crusty bread. Crisp salad. Salty olives. The car starting on the first try. A red carnation sitting jauntily on the desk. Daffodils and paperwhites displayed in the florist's window. Kids laughing as they get off the bus in the afternoon.

L ook and listen. What are the sounds of your life today? The swish of water from a faucet. Silent snow falling on a fast-whitening ground. The crack of icicles in a spring melt. The drone of lawnmowers on a summer afternoon. The clink and tinkle of ice in a glass. Voices murmuring at tables in a restaurant. Frogs croaking by the creek. A child whispering in your ear. Leaves in the wind. A plane flying overhead. Music on the stereo. Sweet silence.

Abundance is . . . having ears open to hear the music of life.

Where you pleasure is, there is your treasure: where your treasure,
there your heart; where your heart, there your happiness.

—SAINT AUGUSTINE

G o ahead. Invest in yourself. Take time to read a book, go to the park, watch a sunset. Buy something that makes you feel special—a small bottle of perfume, a single rose, a favorite magazine. Call a friend and make a date for lunch. Replace your ratty underwear with some new colorful delights. Buy a vase for your desk and a fresh flower at the beginning of each work week. Go buy some gourmet coffee or tea.

I nvest in tomorrow today. Take a class, redecorate your bedroom, read a helpful book, learn a new skill—think in terms of lasting investments that will bring you joy not only in the immediate present but also over the long run.

> *I like living. I have sometimes been wildly, despairingly,*
> *acutely miserable, racked with sorrow, but through it all I still*
> *know quite certainly that just to be alive is a grand thing.*
> —AGATHA CHRISTIE

L et yourself have fun. Go ahead, a little frivolity never killed anyone. (I've heard of worrying oneself into an early grave. But I've never heard anyone say, "She was just so *frivolous* it killed her.")

Now when I say frivolity, I mean the kind of things our work ethic, straight-jacket mind puts down. You know the drill. Your mind says, "What are you doing, taking time to go play with the neighbor's dog? Don't you realize that you can't go out and enjoy this sunny day unless you clean the grout between your bath tiles? You can't enjoy a pretty dress unless your figure is dieted and exercised to an inch of perfection. And really, how frivolous for such a serious-minded go-getter to smell a rose or sit down and read a magazine when there is a corporate ladder to climb."

Get real. Life is a series of little moments. Make the most of your moments by having some lighthearted fun.

The true object of life is play.

—G. K. CHESTERTON

Abundance is . . . a wiggling, tail-wagging puppy.

Abundance is . . . learning how to ride a bike.

Abundance is . . . air conditioning in a hot climate.

Abundance is . . . a pure white seashell
you discover on the beach.

The greatest mistake you can make is to be continually fearing
you will make one.

—ELBERT HUBBARD

Take some risks. Try something new. Don't always play it safe. Whether it's as simple as taking another road home or as complex as going back to school to get your degree, an element of risk is always involved with adventuring into new territory. Don't let life become a boring rut, always doing the same old thing. Did you know that the physical symptoms of fear and excitement are almost exactly the same? Think about that the next time something makes your heart beat faster. Will you choose fear? Or will you choose excitement?

The Celebration of Abundance

The only thing we have to fear is fear itself—
nameless, unreasoning, unjustified terror which paralyzes
needed efforts to convert retreat into advance.
—FRANKLIN DELANO ROOSEVELT

When I am afraid, I put my trust in thee.
—PSALM 56:3 (RSV)

Abundance is . . . the courage to try something new.

C reate special moments now. Sometimes it seems like we spend our lives waiting for tomorrow. "When I get enough money I'll . . . " "When I have a better house I'll . . . " "When I find someone to love I'll . . . " "When I retire I'll . . . " It is so easy to lose sight of the fact that we only have today. There are no guarantees for tomorrow, only promises that God will take care of us.

Abundance is . . . being alone in a crowd, but not lonely.

We die daily. Happy those who daily come to life as well.
—GEORGE MACDONALD

Abundance is . . . inviting people to a party.

Abundance is . . . a party of two anywhere.

Abundance is . . . a class in a subject you're interested in.

Hunger is the best sauce in the world.

—CERVANTES

Abundance is . . . having tea with friends.

*Don't worry about tomorrow. Tomorrow will take
care of itself soon enough. Let what this day brings—
tears or laughter—be what you focus on.*

—MATTHEW 6:34 (AUTHOR'S PARAPHRASE)

Abundance is . . . knitting needles and a ball of yarn.

Abundance is . . . a bicycle, a sunny day, and an open road.

Abundance is . . . trying on hats, just for the fun of it.

W atch young children. When they play, they are entirely in the moment—this ice cream cone, this crayon and paper, this tetherball game, this time with my friends. Children hold nothing back. Look at a toddler learning to walk and discovering the world. Think of a child's eyes on Christmas morning. Give yourself a gift by celebrating the wonders of daily life. You never know what small surprise packages will arrive. Let the little child in your heart become an explorer again.

The Celebration of Abundance

Abundance is . . . wind chimes in a garden.

Abundance is . . . a warm sweater on a cool day.

Abundance is . . . sharing a popsicle.

Abundance is . . . a cherry on top!

Abundance is . . . coffee at a bohemian campus hangout.

Abundance is . . . little girls giggling at a slumber party.

Abundance is . . . the taste of fresh-picked raspberries.

Sometimes I would almost rather have people take away
years of my life than take away a moment.

—PEARL BAILEY

Enjoy the view. Whether the big goal is reached or not, we can enjoy the journey. Make each moment count. Try to be aware of the sensory experiences of existence. Be mindful of the taste, feel, sight, scent, and sound of the things you normally take for granted.

Live as if you were to die tomorrow.

—ISODORE OF SEVILLE

Abundance is . . . a baked apple, fragrant with butter and cinnamon, swimming in cream.

Abundance is . . . the cry of a seagull whirling and wheeling in the wind.

Abundance is . . . the smell of coffee brewing.

My crown is called content, a crown that seldom kings enjoy.
—WILLIAM SHAKESPEARE

The art of the melody can never be put down on paper.

—PABLO CASALS

Abundance is . . . a song in the night.

Abundance is . . . making beautiful music together.

Abundance is . . . a screen door that keeps the bugs out.

Abundance is . . . a cat peering in at you
from the screen door it climbed on.

Abundance is . . . a pot of homemade soup
bubbling on the stove.

Abundance is . . . taking the time to do it right.

Dost thou love life? Then do not squander time,
for that's the stuff life is made of.
—BENJAMIN FRANKLIN

Abundance is . . . decorating a birthday cake with sugar flowers
and "Happy Birthday" written in icing.

Abundance is . . . a lamb frolicking in a meadow.

The best thing about the future is that it
only comes one day at a time.
—ABRAHAM LINCOLN

Abundance is . . . a dewdrop-spangled rose.

Abundance is . . . a little girl in a big red coat with bright
cobalt blue cap and mittens.

Abundance is . . . one small step at a time.

Life is always a rich and steady time when you are
waiting for something to happen or to hatch.
—E. B. WHITE

Abundance is . . . a robin's nest with an egg
that looks like a piece of sky.

Abundance is . . . seeds that sprouted in a clay pot.

O taste and see that the LORD is good!
Happy is the man who takes refuge in him!
—PSALM 34:8 (RSV)

W hen in doubt, believe the best. Whether it is for your future or about the people you know, believing the best brings back the best. It's almost like sending a radio message out to the universe, "You can trust me to appreciate the good gifts you're sending!" A little seed of gratitude can one day grow into a crop of blessings.

Bless the LORD, O my soul; and all that is
within me bless his holy name!
—PSALM 103:1 (RSV)

*Instead of allowing yourself to be so unhappy, just let your love
grow as God wants it to grow; seek goodness in others, love more
persons more; love them more impersonally, more unselfishly, without
thought of return. The return, never fear, will take care of itself.*

—HENRY DRUMMOND

Abundance is . . . enough money for today's bills.

Abundance is . . . the barns at the state fair.

Great men are they who see that spiritual is stronger than
any material force; that thoughts rule the world.
—RALPH WALDO EMERSON

Abundance is . . . a friend who believes in you.

Abundance is . . . sunlight slanting through the trees.

Abundance is . . . rabbits!

Abundance is . . . an organic garden where weeds
and bugs also are allowed to grow.

Abundance is . . . crickets singing in the summer heat.

Abundance is . . . warm cement under
your feet on a cool evening.

C ount your blessings. It's a simple thing to do, but very effective. I write down five things each day to be thankful for. I do this just before bedtime. Even a rough day can have its blessings—sometimes the fact that it's over! I often go back and remind myself of how much I have enjoyed each day and what a privileged being I am to enjoy the gifts God has so richly given.

He who is plenteously provided for from within needs but little from without.

—GOETHE

Abundance is . . . waves washing on a sandy shore.

Abundance is . . . a grateful heart.

A well-spent day brings happy sleep.

—LEONARDO DA VINCI

In peace I will both lie down and sleep; for thou alone,
O LORD, makest me dwell in safety.

—PSALM 4:8 (RSV)

Abundance is . . . the lights of home in the darkness.

D are to fantasize! Dare to think without limitation. Get free and crazy with this. Ask yourself questions like:

If I could do anything for the next 48 hours (no limitations) what would I do? Fly to London and see *The Phantom of the Opera*? Go skin diving in the warm blue seas of Tahiti? Fly to Paris for an elegant dinner? Climb a mountain? Go for a mad shopping spree in the Mall of America? Curl up with a good book and a whole chocolate cake? Discover a cure for cancer?

If I had ten lives to live, what would I be? A ballerina? A fireman? A cowgirl? An interior designer? An Olympic swimming or skating champion? A mad scientist?

Give yourself a part of that fantasy now. Ask yourself what small part of that fantasy can you re-create in your life. You may not be a prima ballerina, but you can buy a ticket to the ballet or take a dance class or read a book on ballerinas. You might not live in Paris, but you can have a cup of coffee and a croissant at a local cafe. If you want to write the Great American Novel but you haven't written more than thank-you notes and grocery lists in the last year, it's time to take a creative writing class at your local community college.

You may find you're satisfied with one small affirming gesture. Or you may discover that one thing will lead to another and launch you on an unexpected adventure that takes you places you never expected to go. A journey can begin with one small step.

D reams of the future offer us clues to what we want in the present. I've lived in many apartments, but I've always dreamed of having a beautiful home with lots of space and gracious decor. So I learned to create little gracious spaces, even when I lived in crowded and tiny apartments. It's good practice for that dream house, and it gives my life the pleasant touches I long for without depending on some future dream.

I would love to dress up and go to the symphony or theater in London. So I dress nicely to go to a friend's house or out to a small club or theater in my home town. I buy season tickets for the symphony in the nosebleed section. I rent a video to learn something more about opera, or Beethoven, or touring London. I don't sit and complain about what I don't have. I create! I look for small fulfillments, incremental joys.

Abundance is . . . playing dress-up with friends of any age.

Abundance is . . . watching professional dancers perform a passionate spectacle of art, discipline, and pure glorious energy.

L isten to music that moves you. Buy season tickets to a concert series or invest in your favorite CDs. Give yourself permission to explore new kinds of music, go to concerts and special events, learn how to play an instrument, join a choir, and take time to give yourself the gift of music.

I am fortunate enough to live in a town where I can go to listen to music any night of the week. Nashville is a music mecca where the best in the world come to play and sing. Not only are there concert headliners, but there are clubs that feature yet-to-be-discovered songwriters and artists. Many, many of these are free. I go out often and enjoy all types of music.

No matter where you live, there is music available somewhere. You can make your own music, too. Enjoy the music of the world that surrounds you—crickets, wind, children, and all the sounds that make life here on earth so rich.

Abundance is . . . an orchestra tuning up.

Abundance is . . . the chuckling of a little brown creek.

You've got to be sold on the subject. I don't know of
a single agnostic or atheist who is a hymnwriter.
—ROBERT J. BATASTINI, EDITOR, G.I.A. PUBLICATIONS
(A RELIGIOUS MUSIC PUBLISHING HOUSE)

Where were you when I laid the foundation of the earth . . . when all the
morning stars sang together, and all the sons of God shouted for joy?
—JOB 38:4 & 7 (RSV)

Abundance is . . . listening to birdsong on an early spring morning.

Abundance is . . . a little girl dancing around the living room
to Beethoven's *Pastoral* Symphony.

*To know of someone here and there whom we
accord with, who is living on with us, even in silence—
this makes our earthly ball a peopled garden.*

—GOETHE

Abundance is . . . your favorite song on the
radio instead of another advertisement.

Abundance is . . . sitting high in the balcony
with a friend and sharing the music.

C lean out your closets. There's nothing like seeing all the stuff you've accumulated to remind you of how much you already have. Give away good used clothing and other useful items to deserving charities. Let someone else enjoy what's been hiding unused in your closet.

Life begets life. Energy creates energy. It is by spending oneself
that we become rich.
—SARAH BERNHARDT

The best way to cheer yourself up is to try to cheer somebody else up
—MARK TWAIN

God loves a cheerful giver.
—II CORINTHIANS 9:7 (AUTHOR'S PARAPHRASE)

Buy one small impractical thing, like a single fresh rose for the table by your bed. For few dollars, you can buy a rose and fern from the grocery store or florist. For the next few days it will remind you of the mystery of growth and change, breathing beauty into your first waking moments and those right before you go to sleep.

Abundance is . . . fresh flowers and
candles on the dinner table.

Abundance is . . . anything chocolate.

Abundance is . . . cotton candy clouds and buttercream skies.

The Art of Abundance

Abundance is . . . a year's subscription to a favorite magazine.

Abundance is . . . a colorful silk scarf that
was too beautiful not to buy.

Abundance is . . . white gloves and pink taffeta.

Abundance is . . . a lighted Christmas tree in a neighbor's window.

This time, like all times, is a very good one
if we but know what to do with it.
—RALPH WALDO EMERSON

Take time to pamper yourself. This is especially important if you spend a great deal of time nurturing others. Your well will run dry if you don't give yourself permission to fill it. Your body needs rest. You need to bathe and wash your hair. Make necessary personal care as much of a luxury experience as you can afford.

You may not be able to take a sensuous bubble bath every day, but as an occasional treat, it can't be beat. Keep packets of bubble bath or bath beads on hand. For a few dollars, you can have the home version of an expensive spa.

Lock the bathroom door. Light some candles. Run the bath water and luxuriate in the scented warmth. You deserve it.

Abundance is . . . water running into the
tub for a fragrant bubble bath.

Abundance is . . . a trip to the hairdresser
for a shampoo, cut, and style.

Abundance is . . . breakfast in bed.

Abundance is . . . a twenty-minute walk in the fresh air.

Abundance is . . . getting your annual checkup.

Abundance is . . . the virgin surface of a
newly opened container of ice cream.

Abundance is . . . a thick towel wrapped around a wet body.

Take time to pamper someone else.

Abundance is . . . a backrub.

Abundance is . . . a thank-you note.

Abundance is . . . bathtub toys for the kids.

Abundance is . . . a rose and an encouraging
card for a friend.

Always be kinder than necessary.
—SIR JAMES BARRIE

One of the most soothing things I did as a child was to write numbers on a page. 1, 2, 3, 4, 5, 6, . . . 101, 102, 103, etc. I'm sure part of it was the feeling of accomplishment, proving to myself that I knew my numbers. But it also gave me a great satisfaction to see the page fill with all those numbers I had written in neat order.

Even as adults we can be soothed by simple repetitious games, like numbering the gifts of creation. On a clear summer night, go out and count the stars. When you've finished, count the fireflies in the grass. Then count the leaves in the trees.

Abundance is . . . a talent contest.

Abundance is . . . a field of ripe corn.

Abundance is . . . counting waves roll in
on an ocean beach.

How precious to me are thy thoughts, O God!
How vast is the sum of them! If I would count them,
they are more than the sand.
Were I to come to the end I would still be with thee.
—PSALM 139:17-18 (RSV)

He prayeth best, who loveth best,
All things both great and small;
For the dear God who loveth us,
He made and loveth all.
—SAMUEL TAYLOR COLERIDGE

The beginning of wisdom is this:
Get wisdom,
and whatever you get, get insight.
—PROVERBS 4:7 (RSV)

There are three ingredients in the good life: learning, earning, and yearning.
—CHRISTOPHER MORELY

Teach us to number our days that we may get a heart of wisdom.
—PSALM 90:12 (RSV)

Abundance is . . . a smile and a wave.

Abundance is . . . pouring tea from a fat, white teapot.

Abundance is . . . having enough to share.

A man wrapped up in himself makes a small bundle.
—BENJAMIN FRANKLIN

The Art of Abundance

I love to think of nature as an unlimited broadcasting station
through which God speaks to us every hour, if we will only tune in.
—GEORGE WASHINGTON CARVER

Abundance is . . . a fish at the end of your line.

Abundance is . . . a long walk down a country road.

Most folks are about as happy as they
make up their minds to be.
—ABRAHAM LINCOLN

Time is an education for eternity.

—ANONYMOUS

Sit and watch the grass grow. There's a popular saying that goes, "Sometimes I sits and thinks. And sometimes I just sits." Sitting still is good for your soul. It is an antidote to the "hurry, hurry, hurry" sickness of our times. Our utilitarian society pressures us to be constantly busy and productive. But the "busy and important" syndrome is death to the human spirit. We are not wired to be constantly on the go.

Start a revolution! Take ten minutes to sit back and let the world soak into your pores. Take a course in the art of "being" by watching cows in a pasture. Stop and listen—you might even hear the voice of God speaking to your heart.

"Sitting 101" is just sitting and being. "Advanced Sitting 202" is praying or meditating. Let your brain drain and give your soul time to breathe.

Be still and know that I am God.

—PSALM 46:10 (RSV)

G o to a bakery. Smell the glorious scent of fresh baked goods. Look at all the different kinds of breads, rolls, pastries. Buy something and take it home to eat.

Abundance is . . . friends who think you're a big cheese when
the rest of the world thinks you're small potatoes.

The Celebration of Abundance

Man is a very comic creature, and most of the things he does
are comic—eating, for instance. And the most comic things of all are
exactly the things that are most worth doing—such as making love.

—G. K. CHESTERTON

Shop at a tourist trap. Go ahead. Don't be ashamed. Pretend you're a tourist in your own home town. Search for the tackiest thing in the store. Look for something clever that you would never have thought of making. Find ideas for discovering special things about your home town (or, if you're visiting somewhere, for discovering new things about a new place).

Abundance is . . . the crack of a bat meeting a ball.

Abundance is . . . a town full of tourist traps
during the tourist season.

V isit a shop that carries spices and herbs or gourmet teas and coffees. Buy an herb or spice to try in a new recipe. Experiment with a new coffee or tea, then share your discovery with a friend or loved one.

Abundance is . . . knowing you can buy
something even if you decide not to.

Abundance is . . . vintage lace.

Were there no God, we would be in this glorious world
with grateful hearts: and no one to thank.
—CHRISTINA GEORGINA ROSSETTI

Abundance is . . . a holiday parade.

Abundance is . . . flags on the Fourth of July.

Know that the LORD is God! It is he that made us, and we are his;
we are his people, and the sheep of his pasture.
—PSALM 100:3 (RSV)

Gather fall leaves. See how many different kinds of leaves you can find. See how many different colors of leaves you can collect. Find a pile of fall leaves to swish your feet through.

Abundance is . . . scissors, glue, and construction paper.

Abundance is . . . a brown speckled trout
swimming in a clear green pond.

Be thankful for the least gift,
so shalt thou be meet to receive greater.
—THOMAS A. KEMPIS

Search for pussywillows in the early spring. Look at frost patterns on a winter window. Carve a jack-o-lantern out of a brilliant orange pumpkin. Play a game of volleyball on a summer lawn. Celebrate the moments that each season brings.

The Art of Abundance

Abundance is . . . Sunday dinner with roast chicken, green peas, mashed potatoes, gravy, and ice cream with chocolate sauce for dessert.

Abundance is . . . getting off work early.

Abundance is . . . a freshly ironed shirt.

Wondrous is the strength of cheerfulness, and its power of endurance—
the cheerful man will do more in the same time, will do it better,
will persevere in it longer, than the sad or sullen.
—THOMAS CARLYLE

Slide down a snowy hillside on a sled or your backside. Roll in the grass on a dry sunny day. Take regular walks outdoors.

Abundance is . . . store windows that
display the delights within.

Abundance is . . . the wind blowing through your hair.

Abundance is . . . zucchini!

P et a dog. Stroke a cat. Put out a birdfeeder in winter. Watch an ant make its way across a sidewalk. Enjoy a nature program that teaches you about the wonders of the animal kingdom.

Abundance is . . . reading *The Tale of Peter Rabbit* to a child.

Abundance is . . . a curious cat.

Abundance is . . . Canada geese in flight.

Abundance is . . . a full dog dish.

Abundance is . . . butterflies against a blue, blue sky.

Consider the birds of the air; they neither sow nor reap
nor gather into barns, and yet your heavenly Father feeds them.
Are you not of more value than they?
—MATTHEW 6:26 (RSV)

L ook through a telescope. A microscope. A kaleidoscope. Put your rose-colored glasses on and seek the beauty, wonder, and wildness of this ever-changing world.

The telescope makes the world smaller;
it is only the microscope that makes it larger.
—G. K. CHESTERTON

Abundance is . . . voices blended in close harmony.

Abundance is . . . bugs around the porchlight in summer.

Abundance is . . . a merry-go-round at a county fair.

Open your eyes and the whole world is full of God.
—JACOB BOEHME

W atch an old Laurel and Hardy movie. Or a Buster Keaton movie. Or a Charlie Chaplin movie. Or a Three Stooges movie. Or a Jerry Lewis movie. Get the picture?

Abundance is . . . a friend to laugh with.

Abundance is . . . ducks on a pond.

Abundance is . . . ducks waddling on land.

Life, it seems to me, is worth living, but only if we avoid
the amusements of grown-up people.
—ROBERT LYND

Then our mouth was filled with laughter, and our
tongues with shouts of joy.
—PSALM 126:2 (RSV)

T ake a walk outdoors. Look at the sky and the passing clouds. Celebrate the seasonal changes. Observe the wonderful variety of nature, of the beautiful creation God set us in.

In those vernal seasons of the year when the air is
calm and pleasant, it were an injury and sullenness
against nature not to go out and see her riches,
and partake in her rejoicing with heaven and earth.

—JOHN MILTON

Abundance is . . . a rainbow arching across the sky.

Oh Lord, that lends me life, lend me a heart replete with thankfulness.
—WILLIAM SHAKESPEARE

It is a good thing to thank the Lord.
—PSALM 92:1 (AUTHOR'S PARAPHRASE)

Abundance is . . . a bride dressed in white.

Abundance is . . . a field of daisies.

Abundance is . . . a lace tablecloth.

Abundance is . . . walking across a campus
on a crisp fall day.

Abundance is . . . the wind in the
sails of a sailboat.

L ook at old photos. Remember the good times. Forgive the mistakes. Thank God for the people He has brought into your life.

Abundance is . . . baskets full of memories.

Abundance is . . . a photo of your parent's wedding.

Abundance is . . . a sepia picture of
Main Street America circa 1909.

R ead a good book.

My favorite books have helped me discover the abundance in life, and many of them have literally been life-transforming for me:

The Hidden Art of Homemaking by Edith Schaeffer

The Supper of the Lamb by Robert Farrar Capon

The Adventure of Living by Paul Tournier

Do What You Love, The Money Will Follow by Marsha Sinetar

The Artist's Way by Julia Cameron

Walking on Water by Madeleine L'Engle

Pilgrim at Tinker Creek by Annie Dillard

Listening to Your Life by Frederick Buechner

A Thomas Merton Reader edited by Thomas P. McDonnell

The Message by Eugene Peterson

Disciplines for the Inner Life by Bob Benson Sr. & Michael W. Benson

The Book of Common Prayer

Gift from the Sea by Anne Morrow Lindbergh

Reflections on the Psalms by C. S. Lewis

A Natural History of the Senses by Diane Ackerman

The Wind in the Willows by Kenneth Grahame

Winnie the Pooh by A. A. Milne

Living a Beautiful Life by Alexandra Stoddard

The Art of Eating by M. F. K. Fisher

Abundance is . . . a shelf packed with your favorite books.

Plant a seed. Plan a garden. Poke a hole in the ground, stick a seed in, and watch it grow. It doesn't matter if you have a tiny pot on an apartment deck or windowsill, or a big old fashioned garden; watching things grow is good therapy for the soul. It reminds us of forces deeper and stronger than us.

Take a trip to a botanical garden or your local plant nursery and revel in all the good growing things. I have a favorite local nursery and florist that has gorgeous displays all year round. It lifts my heart to see a spring garden in the heart of winter—and to buy a pot of paperwhites for my coffee table. The fragrance of spring is sweeter in winter.

Abundance is . . . dandelion seeds.

Abundance is . . . an omelette made with fresh herbs.

Abundance is . . . polishing a silver tea service
and heirloom silver spoons.

Abundance is . . . a planter full of blooming annuals.

My soul can find no staircase to Heaven
unless it be through Earth's loveliness.
—MICHELANGELO

G o to an airport, a mall, a train station, a busy street. Sit down. Watch the parade pass by. Count noses and see how many different noses there are on all the different faces.

Go to the zoo. Look at the animals. Look at the people. Think about God's infinite variety.

Go to the public library. Browse through the books on bugs. The books on boats. The books on fishes and life in the ocean. The books on stars. The cookbooks. The biographies. The crafts section. The literature section. The children's book section. I am always delighted and distracted by all the funny and amazing things people find to write entire books about.

Abundance is . . . homemade fudge.

Abundance is . . . an afternoon in a hammock reading
a trashy novel (admit it, you like a good trash wallow every now and again!).

Subscribe to a favorite magazine. Take the time to read it when it comes each month. I can't wait to relax for a few moments with a magazine that helps me get a wider view of the world.

I have years of back issues of *Victoria*, *Traditional Home*, *Romantic Homes*, *Natural Health*, *Country Gardens*, *European Travel and Life*, *Gourmet*, *Eating Well*, and a special pile of Christmas and holiday magazines of all kinds. Some magazines are now defunct but the old issues are wonderful to reread. If I don't want to save the magazines, I use them for collages and crafts or recycle them.

Abundance is . . . a travel poster that makes you dream of
blue skies, exotic flowers, and faraway places.

Abundance is . . . the swish of taffeta, the sheen of silk.

Abundance is . . . a double mocha latte with
whipped cream and chocolate sprinkles.

Whatever comes, let's be content with all:
Among God's blessings there is no one small.
—ROBERT HERRICK

When you have eaten, and when you are satisfied,
then give God thanks for the fruitful land he's given you.
—DEUTERONOMY 8:10 (AUTHOR'S PARAPHRASE)

Abundance is . . . silver and crystal
shimmering in candlelight.

Splurge! Treat yourself to a wonderful meal at a good local restaurant. Don't forget to read the menu and savor how many delights you have to choose from.

Abundance is . . . trying a new flavor of ice cream.

Don't splurge. Sometimes we fill our lives with too many things, too many activities. Take a day off to simplify. Fast. Don't do any of your usual activities. Don't buy anything. Don't watch TV.

Instead, take time to read or think, to pray or to stare at the clouds as they pass. Take a nap or a walk or just sit. Be quiet. Listen to what your heart says. Read Scripture. Write in your journal. Or be still and watch water ripple in a spring-swollen stream or green grass growing in a summer sun or leaves falling from autumn trees or icicles dripping outside your winter window. Take time to just BE instead of always doing, buying, accomplishing, etc.

Abundance is . . . a hot meal ready to eat.

Abundance is . . . a beckoning trail.

Take a gratitude walk. Thank God for all the good gifts in your life as you walk through forest, field, or town. Let the rhythm of each footstep echo, "Thank you. Thank you."

The Sharing of
Abundance

*You cannot always have happiness, but you can
always give happiness.*

—UNKNOWN

SHARE THE ABUNDANCE

True abundance is love in action. God in his love gives to us. We, in turn, give to others. We can be a part of the chain of love, making a circle of giving that makes its way back around to us in God's good time.

We are made for giving and sharing. True abundance opens its arms to others. Sometimes we get so busy we forget how important being with others can be. Make time in your life for the small joys of giving, sharing, and togetherness.

It must be obvious to those who take time to look at
human life that its greatest values lie not in getting things,
but in doing them, in doing them together, in all working
toward a common aim, in the experience of comradeship,
of warmhearted 100 percent human life.

—W. T. GRANT

Abundance is . . . teaching a child about gardens.

Abundance is . . . a cool hand on a hot forehead.

The races of mankind would perish did they cease to
aid each other. From the time the mother binds the child's
head till the moment that some kind assistant wipes the brow
of the dying, we cannot exist without mutual help.

—SIR WALTER SCOTT

Abundance is . . . offering encouragement
instead of objections.

Abundance is . . . respecting others'
dreams and differences.

*Little progress can be made by merely
attempting to repress what is evil; our great hope
lies in developing what is good.*
—CALVIN COOLIDGE

Abundance is . . . listening to a three-year-old
explain his world to you.

God has given us two hands—one to receive with and
the other to give with. We are not cisterns made for hoarding;
we are channels made for sharing.
—BILLY GRAHAM

Abundance is . . . a warm shoulder in a cold world.

Spend a few hours with a friend, a loved one, or a child. Make a protected time for just the two of you. Do something fun, something relaxing, and something that gives you time and space to talk about life.

Abundance is . . . a tickle and a cuddle.

Abundance is . . . telling stories, enjoying good food,
and sitting around the table laughing.

Giving is the secret of a healthy life. Not necessarily money,
but whatever a man has of encouragement and
sympathy and understanding.
—JOHN D. ROCKEFELLER, JR.

Above all hold unfailing your love for one another,
since love covers a multitude of sins.
—I PETER 4:8 (RSV)

Give what you have. To someone it may be
better than you dare think.
—HENRY WADSWORTH LONGFELLOW

Abundance is . . . the good Samaritan who helped you fix a flat tire.

Abundance is . . . a compliment on how you look.

W rap a present. Buy small gifts to surprise others. Don't wait for birthdays or holidays. Sometimes the most wonderful gifts are the unexpected ones. Give a gift that says, "This isn't because of any obligation, but just because I think you're wonderful."

Abundance is . . . finding the perfect gift for someone you love.

All who would win joy, must share it; happiness was born a twin.
—LORD BYRON

Abundance is . . . a handful of wildflowers.

The Sharing of Abundance

Abundance is . . . children's drawings hanging on the refrigerator door.

Abundance is . . . hugs and kisses at a family reunion.

Abundance is . . . a jigsaw puzzle to put together.

The smallest actual good is better than the
most magnificent promise of impossibilities.
—THOMAS BABINGTON MACAULAY

V olunteer. Give yourself to something that matters. Donate to a good cause or give a few hours of your time to a cause you care about. Ask yourself, "How can I give back?"

Whether it's serving at a soup kitchen, teaching Sunday school, doing a Fun Run to raise money, tutoring students, or knitting socks, we all have something to offer. A friendly, helping hand; an encouraging smile; a willingness to help someone else—all these gifts, when given with no strings attached, bring their own rewards.

The test of our progress is not whether we add more to
the abundance of those who have much; it is whether we provide enough
for those who have too little.
—FRANKLIN D. ROOSEVELT,
SECOND INAUGURAL ADDRESS, JANUARY 20, 1937

For example, one local church is involved with many community projects and ministry outreaches. They co-sponsor a marathon with other area churches to raise funds for the needy. Each year they have donated record-breaking amounts of canned goods for a Thanksgiving food drive. And they financially support a girl's orphanage in Central America, including sending a mission team every year to help build facilities and work with the girls.

If you want to be involved, there are many opportunities. Many churches are involved in such projects, and community organizations need your help, too.

Be not anxious about what you have,
but about what you are.
—SAINT GREGORY THE GREAT

One of my songwriting buddies used to include opportunities to sponsor a child whenever she did concerts. Many people now sponsor children with a monthly donation because my friend cared enough to introduce them to a responsible organization that makes a real difference in third world countries.

How can you find original ways to give?

Kindness is the language which the deaf can hear and the blind can see.

—MARK TWAIN

The constant barrage of news stories of great need and difficult situations around the world can feel overwhelming. Instead of being overwhelmed by all the unmet needs, let God guide your heart to give in your corner of the world. A moderate donation of money, an encouraging word to a friend, or an hour a week volunteering for Traveler's Aid—each small gift is more important than you realize. And many people giving small gifts make a very big difference.

There are many ways to give at home and abroad. Volunteering is a rewarding way to share out of the abundance of your heart.

We cannot live only for ourselves. A thousand fibers connect us
with our fellow men; and along those fibers, as sympathetic threads,
our actions run as causes, and they come back to us as effects.
—HERMAN MELVILLE

Abundance is . . . a full glass of ice water.

Give, and it will be given to you; good measure, pressed down,
shaken together, running over, will be put into your lap.
For the measure you give will be the measure you get back.
—LUKE 6:38 (RSV)

Abundance is . . . a Christmas food drive.

Of all earthly music that which reaches farthest into
heaven is the beating of a truly loving heart.

—HENRY WARD BEECHER

Abundance is . . . all the different faces we see every day.

Abundance is . . . bedtime stories for children.

The liberal man will be enriched,
and one who waters will himself be watered.

—PROVERBS 11:25 (RSV)

Hold a clothing exchange party. It's a great way to clean out your closets, share with others, and have a good time. Three of us hosted such a party. We invited three friends apiece and told everyone to dress for tea and bring useable clothing and accessories to give away.

When the day of the party arrived, we laid out an afternoon tea table and awaited our guests. As each one came in the door, we took their donations and displayed them in another room. (You can purchase racks so that everyone can look through the clothing easily. It almost feels like shopping.) After everyone had an opportunity to get acquainted and to check out the clothing, the exchange began. We had a volunteer hold up each item, like an auctioneer.

By the end of the party, everyone had something to take home, and the unclaimed clothing was donated to a women's organization. It was a great way to get to know new people and help others. I not only cleaned out my closet, I ended up with three "new" dresses to wear!

The Sharing of Abundance

A joy that's shared is a joy made double.

—ENGLISH PROVERB

Abundance is . . . high heels for a very special occasion.

Abundance is . . . a wink and a smile from a
handsome man (or a pretty woman).

Our most valuable possessions are those which can be
shared without lessening—those which, when shared, multiply.
Our least valuable possessions, on the other hand,
are those which, when divided, are diminished.

—WILLIAM H. DANFORTH

Abundance is . . . giving a friend room to grow.

Abundance is . . . a lighthouse defying the
restless sea and guiding the traveler home.

There is an idea abroad among moral people
that they should make their neighbors good. One person
I have to make good: Myself. But my duty to my
neighbor is much more nearly expressed by saying
that I have to make him happy if I may.
—ROBERT LOUIS STEVENSON

Love is patient and kind;
love is not jealous or boastful;
it is not arrogant or rude.
Love does not insist on its own way;
it is not irritable or resentful;
it does not rejoice at wrong
but rejoices in the right.
—I CORINTHIANS 13:4-6 (RSV)

Write a thank-you note or a letter to someone who mentored you or taught you or helped you along the way. Let that person know what he or she has meant in your life.

When someone does something good, applaud!
You will make two people happy.
—SAMUEL GOLDWYN

Abundance is . . . having someone say,
"Yes, you can!" instead of "Yes, but . . . "

The Sharing of Abundance

Abundance is . . . good memories.

The best portion of a good man's life,
His little, nameless, unremembered acts
Of kindness and of love.
—WILLIAM WORDSWORTH

rite an encouraging letter or call a friend who needs to know that you care and that you believe in them.

Abundance is . . . someone to walk along
the path with you for awhile.

Abundance is . . . a funny card.

Abundance is . . . a friend to laugh with.

The greatest thing a man can do for his Heavenly Father
is to be kind to some of His other children.
—HENRY DRUMMOND

Be kind to one another, tenderhearted,
forgiving one another . . .
—EPHESIANS 4:32 (RSV)

Abundance is . . . someone who cares
enough to worry about you.

Abundance is . . . pictures of family and friends.

Abundance is . . . a mother cuddling her daughter.

Abundance is . . . a father playing catch with his son.

It is astonishing how little one feels poverty when one loves.
—JOHN BULWER

Even a child makes himself known by his acts,
whether what he does is pure and right.
—PROVERBS 20:11 (RSV)

Abundance is . . . having a choice.

Abundance is . . . an understanding friend.

Abundance is . . . having a shoulder to cry on.

Abundance is . . . being a shoulder for
someone else to cry on.

God evidently does not intend us all to be rich, or powerful,
or great, but He does intend us all to be friends.

—RALPH WALDO EMERSON

Resolved, to live with all my might while I do live . . .
Resolved, never to do anything which I should despise or think
meanly of in another. Resolved, never to do anything out of revenge.
Resolved, never to do anything which I should be afraid
to do if it were the last hour of my life.

—JONATHAN EDWARDS

There is gold, and abundance of costly stones;
but the lips of knowledge are a precious jewel.

—PROVERBS 20:15 (RSV)

Abundance is . . . the first football practice in August.

Abundance is . . . a sympathetic friend to listen and
pick up the pieces when you fall apart.

Abundance is . . . a cloud with silver linings.

Abundance is . . . a full punchbowl.

Abundance is . . . the little wild roses that
grow near a saltwater beach.

Abundance is . . . helping a toddler explore the world.

Abundance is . . . a golden wedding anniversary.

The fragrance of what you give away stays with you.
—EARL ALLEN

One man gives freely, yet grows all the richer; another withholds what he should give and only suffers want.

—PROVERBS 11:24 (RSV)

Abundance is . . . rubbing noses as a sign of affection.

I never knew how to worship until I knew how to love.

—HENRY WARD BEECHER

The Discovery of Abundant Living

In spite of illness, in spite even of the archenemy sorrow, one can remain alive long past the usual date of disintegration if one is unafraid of change, insatiable in intellectual curiosity, interested in big things, and happy in small ways.

—EDITH WHARTON

THE ABUNDANT LIFE

Life is not a march, it's a dance!

Sometimes I'll find myself looking at life as if it is some big formula that I must solve. In so doing, I turn life into a march when it is meant to be a dance. Life is not neat columns of soldiers marching in lockstep to a prescribed order but an elegant interweaving of free choice and adherance to an ordered, yet changing, pattern. It is couples waltzing round the floor, dresses swirling, toes tapping, hearts singing. It is moving together, then apart, then together again in an exquisite movement that is as natural as breathing in and out. Changing tempo, adjusting steps, learning new intricate combinations of patterns, whirling round the room with joy and lightness and laughter—we dance to the music of life. It's a social grace, not military order.

Watch trees sway in the wind, or kittens playing, or a brook babbling under a bridge. Listen to the music of life, watch the earth turn through the seasons. Even our very molecules dance with being. Dr. Candace Pert, a neuroscientist who has been in the forefront of biomolecular research, says about the receptor molecules of cells, "We like to describe these receptors as 'keyholes,' although that is not altogether a precise term for something that is constantly moving, dancing in a rhythmic, vibratory way."*

Life is rich, complex, and mysterious. Celebrate the organized chaos of choice, energy, and simple elegance that makes up the dance of life. We are more than the sum of our parts.

> *And David danced before the LORD with all his might . . .*
> —II SAMUEL 6:14 (KJV)

*Candace B. Pert, Ph.D., *The Molecules of Emotion: Why You Feel the Way You Feel,* © 1997, Scribner, pg. 23.

Abundance is . . . the whisper of trees
swaying in a summer breeze.

We carry within us the wonders we seek without us.
—SIR THOMAS BROWNE

Let them praise his name in the dance:
let them sing praises unto him with the timbrel and harp.
—PSALM 149:3 (KJV)

The reason angels can fly is that they
take themselves so lightly.

—G. K. CHESTERTON

The picture of the mind revives again:
While here I stand, not only with the sense
Of present pleasure, but with pleasing thoughts
That in this moment there is life and food
For future years.

—WILLIAM WORDSWORTH

The Discovery of Abundant Living

Abundance is . . . the incomparable perfume of sunshine, fresh air, salt water, and Western Red Cedar and Douglas Fir forest.

Abundance is . . . a morning to sleep in.

Abundance is . . . something wonderful to get up early for.

Abundance is . . . a pencil flying across a piece of paper as words and ideas spill and tumble out.

Abundance is . . . a Mona Lisa smile.

The Art of Abundance

I discovered the art of abundance through a combination of events and people in my life. Several of my songwriting friends and I were working through a book called *The Artist's Way*, by Julia Cameron. In one chapter she talks about recovering a sense of abundance.

I had coffee one day with my gifted friend Donna Michael, a musician and artist who was also working through *The Artist's Way*. She suggested that we have an abundance party. By the time we were done with coffee, we had agreed to call 1995 the Year of Abundance. So in spring of 1995 she and I and Dwight Liles, another gifted songwriting buddy, spent a sunny afternoon at Cheekwood, a beautiful botanical garden and mansion/art gallery in the Nashville area.

T hough all of us were very busy and struggling financially, we felt it was important to take the time off to do this. After strolling the gardens and wandering through art galleries, we enjoyed tea at the Pineapple Room. I have photos to commemorate the day.

Though much of the abundance we desired had yet to arrive, we could celebrate the abundance that already existed—the beauty of the day, the joys of our creativity, and the strength of our encouraging friendship. By the end of the afternoon we were convinced that we were abundantly rich in the things that really matter.

Abundance is . . . friends who share the same dreams and goals.

But that was not the end of abundance for me. Instead, it got me thinking. And then a professional assignment gave me another key. I had done some brainstorming on a subject for a client and realized that making phrases up and playing with words and ideas were my forte. I found myself one afternoon writing pages and pages of "Abundance is . . . " ideas. Gradually those ideas grew into this book.

E ach year since has celebrated and honored, beginning with the year of abundance in 1995. I've enjoyed a year of open doors, a year of prosperity, and a year of joyous discovery. But even in a year of sorrow and loss, I have come to see that a secret gift of abundance is hidden in the darkness, like a seed waiting to awaken to new life. Sometimes the most difficult and painful times clear the way for the birth of something new and wonderful. When I practice the art of abundance, all my days and years have the potential to be fruitful and good.

My times are in thy hands . . .
—PSALM 31:15 (KJV)

We all find time to do what we really want to do.

—WILLIAM FEATHER

Give yourself the gift of time. Time alone, time with friends and loved ones, time to do something you love, and time to grow. Sometimes our minds know the changes we need to make but our hearts haven't made the transition yet. Like a garden through the year, understand that you, too, have your seasons of growth and your seasons of rest. Be patient with yourself and with God. Believe me, he will make your garden grow.

Celebrate what you can do and be patient with what you can't do. Trust that all will work out and that even delays may be part of the plan. You don't have to do everything at once. Take baby steps. Not giant leaps. And let your heart lead the way.

To plow is to pray—to plant is to prophesy,
and the harvest answers and fulfills.
—R. G. INGERSOLL

Abundance is . . . terra cotta urns full of pink geraniums and
blue ageratum flanking the entrance to your home.

Abundance is . . . ripe southern peaches
dripping with juice and flavor.

Abundance is . . . kissing a baby's cheek.

I will bless the LORD at all times:
his praise shall continually be in my mouth.
—PSALM 34:1 (KJV)

One ought, every day at least, to hear a little song,
read a good poem, see a fine picture, and, if it were possible,
to speak a few reasonable words.
—GOETHE

Abundance is . . . a frog choir singing in the swamp.

Abundance is . . . the sun going down
like a ball of fire in the west.

There is no duty we so much underrate
as the duty of being happy.
—ROBERT LOUIS STEVENSON

Abundance is . . . kids in a toy store.

Abundance is . . . the funny names of small towns—
Bucksnort, Puyallup, Twisp, George (Washington state),
Red Boiling Springs, Hungry Horse, Tallapoosa, Boring,
Humptulips—delightful and idiosyncratic names that
celebrate or commemorate stories and people
and dreams and experiences.

Abundance is . . . a Japanese garden.

Abundance is . . . the first crisp day of fall.

Abundance is . . . meeting a friend for
an evening get-together.

Abundance is . . . freshman orientation day
on a green, green campus.

Abundance is . . . the music of "Pomp and Circumstance" as
graduates parade up the aisle to receive their diplomas.

Abundance is . . . peeling enough
apples to make a pie.

The Discovery of Abundant Living

Sing to the LORD with thanksgiving;

make melody to our God upon the lyre!

He covers the heavens with clouds,

he prepares the rain for the earth,

he makes grass grow upon the hills.

—PSALM 147:7-8 (RSV)

It all goes by so fast . . . Oh earth, you're too wonderful

for anybody to realize you . . . Do any human beings ever

realize life while they live it—every, every minute?

—THORNTON WILDER, *OUR TOWN*

Some people despise the little things in life.
It is their mistake, for they thus prevent themselves from
getting God's greatness out of these little things.
—MEISTER ECKHART

Abundance is . . . the bend of a bird wing.

Abundance is . . . a slice of Death by Chocolate cake
(three kinds of chocolate in one sinfully rich dessert).

Abundance is . . . rain after a long dry spell.

The Discovery of Abundant Living

Man is meant for happiness and this happiness is in him,
in the satisfaction of the daily needs of his existence.

—LEO TOLSTOY

Abundance is . . . laugh lines instead of frown lines in an older face.

Abundance is . . . a sunny day picnic in the park.

Abundance is . . . a place to put your feet up and relax.

The Art of Abundance

Abundance is . . . a healthy young woman
in a bright yellow dress.

Abundance is . . . a flag popping in the wind.

All happiness depends on courage and work.
I have had many periods of wretchedness, but with energy,
and above all, with illusions, I pulled through them all.
—HONORÉ DE BALZAC

Abundance is . . . lights twinkling around
the neighborhood at dusk.

The happiest life, seen in perspective, can hardly be better
than a stringing together of odd little moments.
—NORMAN DOUGLAS

Abundance is . . . hot chocolate after playing in the snow.

Abundance is . . . the head of someone you
love on the pillow next to you.

Abundance is . . . sand between your toes.

Abundance is . . . a little one to tuck in at night.

Nine requisites for contented living:

Health enough to make work a pleasure. Wealth enough to support your needs. Strength to battle with difficulties and overcome them. Grace enough to confess your sins and forsake them. Patience enough to toil until some good is accomplished. Charity enough to see some good in your neighbor. Love enough to move you to be useful and helpful to others. Faith enough to make real the things of God. Hope enough to remove all anxious fears concerning the future.

—GOETHE

Abundance is . . . someone saying "yes" to your request.

Abundance is . . . a dog and two kids rolling in the grass.

There is the music of Heaven in all things.
—HILDEGARD OF BINGEN

Abundance is . . . running through the sprinkler.

Abundance is . . . a bowl of Mom's potato salad.

Only those who have the patience to do simple things perfectly
will acquire the skill to do difficult things easily.
—JOHANN VON SCHILLER

Do you see a man skilful in his work? He will stand before kings;
he will not stand before obscure men.
—PROVERBS 22:29 (RSV)

Every good endowment and every perfect gift is from above,
coming down from the Father of lights with whom there is
no variation or shadow due to change.
—JAMES 1:17 (RSV)

If you are content, you have enough to live comfortably.

—PLAUTUS

Abundance is . . . a collection of anything (seashells, baseball cards, perfume bottles, books, bottle caps, antique nutcrackers, stamps—you name it, someone collects it).

Abundance is . . . when the ball goes in the hole, the cup, or the basket.

Abundance is . . . a kitten sleeping on a pillow.

The Art of Abundance

Abundance is . . . a Thanksgiving turkey just out of the oven.

Abundance is . . . the gifts and the potential God has given you.

The future belongs to those who believe in the beauty of their dreams.
—ELEANOR ROOSEVELT

Abundance is . . . a freshly sharpened pencil.

Finally, brethren, whatever is true, whatever is honorable,
whatever is just, whatever is pure, whatever is lovely,
whatever is gracious, if there is any excellence, if there is anything
worthy of praise, think about these things.

—PHILIPPIANS 4:8 (RSV)

Difficult times have helped me to understand
better than before how infinitely rich and beautiful life is
in every way and that so many things that one goes
worrying about are of no importance whatsover.

—ISAK DINESEN

Abundance is . . . little kids in Halloween costumes.

Abundance is . . . fresh basil and summer tomatoes.

Abundance is . . . wind blowing through your hair.

Abundance is . . . a plane twinkling across a purple night sky.

Abundance is . . . the first bite of supper when you're hungry.

God is so humble, he totally hides himself within creation.

—SUFI SAYING

We were given appetites, not to consume the world and forget it,
but to taste its goodness and hunger to make it great.

—ROBERT FARRAR CAPON

The Spirit and the Bride say, "Come."
And let him who hears say, "Come."
And let him who is thirsty come,
let him who desires take the water of life without price.
—REVELATION 22:17 (RSV)

I am still learning.
—MICHELANGELO

Those who dwell among the beauties and mysteries of the
earth are never alone or weary of life.
—RACHEL CARSON

The Discovery of Abundant Living

Abundance is . . . a young smiling girl in a pink jacket.

Abundance is . . . bare branches against a winter sky.

Abundance is . . . cherry cheeks and rosy noses.

For everything that lives is holy; life delights in life.
—WILLIAM BLAKE

Abundance is . . . a cheery hello.

Abundance is . . . music in the distance.

The best friends are those who know how to keep the same silences.
—BISHOP FULTON J. SHEEN

Abundance is . . . a smile from a perfect stranger.

Abundance is . . . golden maple leaves carpeting a forest floor.

Abundance is . . . a jack-o-lantern grinning at you from a doorstep.

Abundance is . . . a comfortable chair.

Abundance is . . . a cat purring in your lap.

Abundance is . . . weeds and wild things.

Abundance is . . . little kids and mud puddles.

Abundance is . . . snowflakes in a snowstorm.

Abundance is . . . the potential of every child born on this earth.

Don't worry about tomorrow, for tomorrow will take care of itself.
Each day has its own challenges to face.
—MATTHEW 6:34 (AUTHOR'S PARAPHRASE)

Think of all the beauty still left around you and be happy.
—ANNE FRANK

Today is for itself enough . . .
—MARY SHELLEY

Abundance is . . . the graceful curve of a fragrant white lily.

The Discovery of Abundant Living

*Be alert for the unpredicted presence of God unexpectedly
intruding upon your everyday life.*

Praise God from whom all blessings flow
Praise Him all creatures here below
Praise Him above ye heavenly host
Praise Father, Son, and Holy Ghost
Amen

About the Author

Candy Paull is the author of *The Art of Simplicity*, *The Art of Abundance*, *The Art of Encouragement*, and *Christmas Abundance*.

Candy's open approach to spirituality draws insight and wisdom from many spiritual traditions, emphasizing that there is something within us that is trustworthy, whole, and wise. Through words and music, she takes complex concepts like grace, truth, goodness, beauty, sacredness, holiness, love, and mercy, and translates them into quiet wisdom that nourishes and enriches daily life.

Candy speaks, sings, and facilitates retreats that combine movement, music, readings, aromatherapy, and other healing modalities to help men and women reduce stress, enjoy a more creative and abundant life, and nurture spiritual growth by integrating body, mind, and spirit. She also speaks at conferences, seminars, and corporate events, and may be contacted at www.candypaull.com.

Candy would like to thank Stephany Evans, Marisa Bulzone, Sara Fortenberry, Rebecca Currington, Frank DeMarco, and Donna Michael for their help and encouragement in the creation of this book.